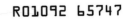

THEY'VE DISCOVERED A HEAD IN THE BOX FOR THE BREAD

and Other Laughable Limericks

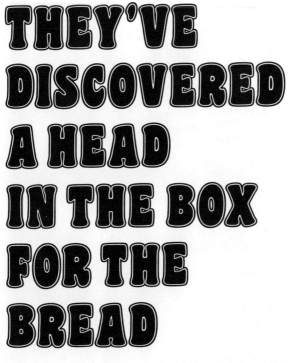

THEY'VE DISCOVERED A HEAD IN THE BOX FOR THE BREAD

and Other Laughable Limericks

COLLECTED BY

John E. Brewton AND *Lorraine A. Blackburn*

ILLUSTRATED BY FERNANDO KRAHN

THOMAS Y. CROWELL · NEW YORK

Copyright © 1978 by John E. Brewton and Lorraine A. Blackburn
All rights reserved. Except for use in a review,
the reproduction or utilization of this work in
any form or by any electronic, mechanical, or
other means, now known or hereafter invented,
including xerography, photocopying, and recording,
and in any information storage and retrieval
system is forbidden without the written permission
of the publisher. Published simultaneously in
Canada by Fitzhenry & Whiteside Limited, Toronto.
Designed by Harriett Barton
Manufactured in the United States of America

Library of Congress Cataloging in Publication Data
Main entry under title:
They've discovered a head in the box for the bread.
SUMMARY: A collection of limericks by different authors.   1. Limericks—Juvenile literature.
[1. Limericks]   I. Brewton, John Edmund.   II. Krahn, Fernando.
PN6231.L5T54   821'.08   77-26598
ISBN 0-690-01388-4   ISBN 0-690-03883-6 lib. bdg.

First Edition

ACKNOWLEDGMENTS

Grateful acknowledgment is made to the following publishers, authors,
and other copyright holders for permission to reprint copyrighted material. Every effort has been made to trace the ownership of copyrighted
material. In the event of errors, the editors will be glad to make the
necessary corrections in future editions of this book.

ATHENEUM PUBLISHERS for "Leaning on a Limerick" by Eve Merriam
from It Doesn't Always Have to Rhyme by Eve Merriam, copyright ©

CONTENTS

Well, it's partly the shape of the thing
That gives the old limerick wing;
    These accordion pleats,
    Full of airy conceits,
Take it up like a kite on a string.

LEANING ON A LIMERICK

from LEANING ON A LIMERICK

Let the limerick form be rehoised
In New Yorkish accents well voiced:
　　"The thoid line is short,
　　And so is the fourt',
While the fi't' and the second go foist."

—Eve Merriam

Lim'ricks and Puns

I'm bored to extinction with Harrison
His lim'ricks and puns are embarrassin'.
    But I'm fond of the bum
    For, though dull as they come,
He makes me seem bright by comparison!

—*Author Unknown*

The Shubble

    There was an old man said, "I fear
    That life, my dear friends, is a bubble,
Still, with all due respect to a Philistine ear,
    A limerick's best when it's double."
    When they said, "But the waste
    Of time, temper, taste!"
He gulped down his ink with cantankerous haste,
    And chopped off his head with a shubble.

—*Walter de la Mare*

Hail to the Town of Limerick

All hail to the town of Limerick
Which provides a cognomen, generic,
    For a species of verse
    Which far better, or worse,
Is supported by layman and cleric.

—Langford Reed

Leaning on a Limerick

Let the limerick form be rehoised
In New Yorkish accents well voiced:
    "The thoid line is short,
    And so is the fourt',
While the fi't' and the second go foist."

2.

When a limerick line starts out first,
What follows is fated, accursed:
    If the third line takes tea,
    The fourth must agree,
While five, two, and one pool their thirst.

3.

Assiduously I'm attending
The limerick message I'm sending;
 I can get up to here,
 But alas and oh dear:
Now what do I do for an ending?

4.

You've a hunger to be newly-versed;
There are rhymes you would dare if you durst:
 Macaroni, baloney,
 Spumoni, tortoni—
But it's got to come out liverwurst.

—*Eve Merriam*

OF CREATURES AND PEOPLE— CAPRICIOUS AND PECULIAR

A Young Lady of Ealing

There was a young lady of Ealing,
Who had a peculiar feeling
That she was a fly,
And wanted to try
To walk upside down on the ceiling.

—Author Unknown

The 'Skeeter and Peter

(A Touching Limerick)

There was a bright fellow named Peter,
Who struck at an active young 'skeeter,
   But the 'skeeter struck first
   And slackened his thirst,
For the 'skeeter was fleeter than Peter.

—Marie Bruckman MacDonald

Tall

So tall was a cowboy called Slouch
He was taller than most in a crouch.
   When a horse stomped his toe,
   Pain had so far to go,
Slouch three days later said, "Ouch!"

—Author Unknown

Suppressed

There was a young fellow named West
Who dreamed he was being suppressed;
   And when he woke up he
   Discovered a puppy
Had fallen asleep on his chest.

—Author Unknown

The Sultan

The Sultan got sore at his harem
And invented a scheme for to scare 'em;
   He caught him a mouse
   Which he loosed in the house;
(The confusion is called harem-scarem).

—Author Unknown

Hog-Calling

A vigorous matron of Baxter
Maintains that hog-calling's relaxter.
   Does it bring home the bacon?
   Her husband (from Macon)
Just shrugs and says, "I never axter."

                 —Roy Blount, Jr.

Hog-Calling Competition

A bull-voiced young fellow of Pawling
Competes in the meets for hog-calling;
   The people applaud,
   And the judges are awed,
But the hogs find it simply appalling.

                 —Morris Bishop

The Surgeon and the Ape

A surgeon once owned a big ape,
He kept it tied up with a tape,
   One day it broke loose
   And stirred up the deuce,
But the surgeon cut off his escape.

                —Author Unknown

The Disobliging Bear

There once was a man who said, "Oh,
Please, good Mr. Bear, let me go;
    Don't you think that you can?"
    The bear looked at the man,
And calmly responded, "Why, no!"

—*Carolyn Wells*

The Thoroughbred Horse

"I have often been told," said the horse,
"Of man's intellectual force,
    A thing, if correct,
    I should never suspect
From the people I meet at the course."

—*Oliver Herford*

Food for a Cat

There was a young lady whose dream
Was to feed a black cat on whipped cream;
    But the first cat she found
    Spilled the cream on the ground,
So she fed a whipped cat on black cream.

—*David Starr Jordan*

9

G Is for Gustave

G is for dear little Gustave,
Who said that a monkey he must have;
   But his parents said not,
   For they thought they had got
All the monkey they wanted in Gustave.

              —*Isabel Frances Bellows*

Nature and Art

Said a lady who wore a swell cape,
As she viewed a rhinoceros, agape,
   "To think in this age
   A beast in a cage
Is permitted our fashions to ape!"

Thought the beast in the cage, "I declare,
One would think that these ladies so fair
   Who come to the zoo
   Have nothing to do
But copy the things that I wear!"

              —*Oliver Herford*

Tact

Quoth a cat to me once: "Pray relieve
My suspense. What does eight from nine
    leave?"
  Poor Puss looked so cold
  And so thin and so old,
I replied, *"Quite a few, I believe."*

                —Oliver Herford

The Panda

A lady who lived in Uganda
Was outrageously fond of her panda:
  With her Chinchilla cat,
  It ate grasshopper fat
On an air-conditioned veranda.

              —William Jay Smith

THE TROUPIAL AND OTHER DISTINGUISHED BEASTS

A Troupial

An unusual thing called a Troupial
Is distinct from a fish or marsupial.
It will stand on two legs
And will always lay eggs
Which no kangaroo, 'possum or guppy'll.

—Milton Bracker

A Beggarly Bear

B was a beggarly bear,
Who carefully curled his front hair;
    He said, "I would buy
    A red-spotted tie,—
But I haven't a penny to spare."

—*Carolyn Wells*

A Corpulent Pig

A cold had a corpulent pig
Who apologized saying, "This thig
    Id by dose
    Distrubs by repose
Ad wodt let be taste, shell or sig!"

—*Marnie and Harnie Wood*

An Ossified Oyster

O was an ossified oyster,
Who decided to enter a cloister.
    He could not return,
    So continued to yearn
For his home in the sea, which was moister.

—*Carolyn Wells*

The Skunk to the Gnu

Said a saucy young skunk to a gnu,
"You are quite odoriferous; phew!"
    Said the gnu to the skunk:
    "If I stank like you stunk
I'd hate to be me, were I you."

—Gerard Neyroud

The Feminine Seal

Said a lachrymose Labrador seal,
When asked why she wept with such zeal,
    "My tears are not lost,
    In this antarctic frost:
To magnificent pearls they congeal."

—Oliver Herford

The Happy Hyena

There once was a happy hyena
Who played on an old concertina.
    He dressed very well
    And in his lapel,
He carelessly stuck a verbena.

—Carolyn Wells

The Exclusive Old Oyster

There was an exclusive old oyster
Who spent all his life in a cloister
   He said, "For a cell
   I prefer my own shell."
That very retiring old oyster.

—Laura A. Steel

The Genial Grimalkin

There was an old cat named Macduff
Who could joke till you cried, "Hold,
    enough!"
   His wife and his child
   So persistently smiled
That their cheeks got a permanent puff.

—J. G. Francis

A Shaggy Dog

There was a small maiden named Maggie,
Whose dog was enormous and shaggy,
   The front end of him
   Looked vicious and grim—
But the tail end was friendly and waggy.

—Author Unknown

Howard

There was a young puppy called Howard,
When at fighting was rather a coward;
   He never quite ran
   When the battle began,
But he started at once to bow-wow hard.

           —A. A. Milne

The Elephant and the Giraffe

Said the elephant to the giraffe,
"Your neck is too long by one half."
   He replied, "Since your nose
   Reaches down to your toes,
At others you'd better not laugh."

           —Charlotte Osgood Carter

ANIMAL ANTICS

The Oratorical Crab

Said the crab: " 'Tis not beauty or birth
That is needed to conquer the earth.
  To win in life's fight,
  First be sure you are right,
Then go sidewise for all you are worth."

—Oliver Herford

The Fastidious Yak

There was once a fastidious yak
Who refused to eat hay from a stack.
　　"A haystack," said he,
　　"Looks so very like me!"
(The haystack's the one at the back.)

—*Oliver Herford*

The Refractory Gnu

It was a refractory gnu,
Which in circus made such a tu du,
　　That the mate to the boss
　　Said, "It may be a loss,
But we must give our gnu to some zu."

—*Author Unknown*

Ballet

A hippo decided one day
That she would take up ballet,
　　So she stood on her toes
　　And said, "Okay, here goes!"
And fell back with a splash in the bay.

—*Author Unknown*

The Bored Ostrich

An ostrich who lived at the zoo
Was bored with nothing to do.
  So he talked a thrush
  Into serving as brush . . .
And painted himself a bright blue.

—Author Unknown

The Sensitive Cat

There once was a sensitive cat
Who couldn't abide the word "Scat."
  "If you want me to go,"
  She yowled, "Say so, you know,
But don't be so rude as all that!"

—*Alice Brown*

The Scholastic Mouse

Said the mouse with scholastical hat,
"I will study the subject of cat!"
  But when puss gave a yawn
  Mr. Mousie was gone
Much quicker than you could say "Scat!"

—*A. B. P.*

The Old Lady from Dover

There was an old lady of Dover
Who baked a fine apple turnover.
  But the cat came that way,
  And she watched with dismay
The overturn of her turnover.

—*Carolyn Wells*

21

The Merry Crocodile

Oh, there once was a merry crocodile;
He was noted on the Ganges for his smile!
   With a very cordial grin
   He would take the natives in—
Oh, this tearful, snaky, smiling crocodile!

                         —*Gertrude E. Heath*

The Dizzy Giraffe

Jerome was a dizzy giraffe
Who put on a disguise for a laugh.
   Well, Jerome was too tall,
   Or the disguise was too small.
Did it cover Jerome? Only half!

                     —*Author Unknown*

An Elephant Sat on Some Kegs

An elephant sat on some kegs,
And juggled glass bottles and eggs,
   And he said "I surmise
   This occasions surprise,—
But, oh dear, how it tires one's legs!"

                     —*J. G. Francis*

Double Entendre

A woodchuck who'd chucked lots of wood
Gave up the hard work, and for good
  For as fast as he'd chuck it
  Some other chuck tuck it
Wooden you give up also? I would.

—J. F. Wilson

The Conservative Owl

A canary, its woe to assuage,
Once invented a wireless cage.
  The owl shook his head,
  "It's a great thought," he said,
"But it's far in advance of the age."

—Oliver Herford

The Kind Armadillo

There once was a kind armadillo,
Who solaced a lone weeping willow.
  Said he: "Do not weep!
  What you need is some sleep;
Pray rest on my shell as a pillow."

—Oliver Herford

The Crocodile

A crocodile once dropped a line
To a fox to invite him to dine;
   But the fox wrote to say
   He was dining, that day,
With a bird friend, and begged to decline.

She sent off at once to a goat.
"Pray don't disappoint me," she wrote;
   But he answered too late,
   He'd forgotten the date,
Having thoughtlessly eaten her note.

The crocodile thought him ill-bred,
And invited two rabbits instead;
   But the rabbits replied,
   They were hopelessly tied
By a previous engagement, and fled.

Then she wrote in despair to some eels,
And begged them to "drop in" to meals;
   But the eels left their cards
   With their coldest regards,
And took to what went for their heels.

Cried the crocodile then, in disgust,
"My motives they seem to mistrust.
    Their suspicions are base,
    Since they don't know their place—
I suppose if I *must* starve, I *must!*"

—*Oliver Herford*

FUNNY FOLK—FRIVOLOUS AND FRENZIED

An Old Looney

There was an old looney of Rhyme
Whose candor was simply sublime:
When they asked, "Are you there?"
He said, "Yes, but take care,
For I'm never 'all there' at a time!"

—Author Unknown

The King

A king, on assuming his reign,
Exclaimed with a feeling of peign;
   "Tho I'm legally heir
   No one here seems to ceir
That I haven't been born with a breign."

—Author Unknown

The Autograph Bore

A is the autograph bore
Whom authors so loudly deplore.
   Tho' it's probably quite,
   If the dears ceased to write,
They'd deplore even more than before.

           —Oliver Herford

A Young Fellow from Boise

There was a young fellow from Boise
Who at times was exceedingly noise.
   So his friends' joy increased
   When he moved way back east
To what people in Brooklyn called Joise.

           —John Straley

A Grumbler Gruff

G is a grumbler gruff
Whom everybody puts in a huff;
   If perchance he shall gain
   Heaven's gate he'll complain
Of his halo or harp like enough.

           —Oliver Herford

Beatnik Limernik

There was a young man with a beard
Who said, "It is just as I feared:
　　If I showered and shaved
　　I'd look just as depraved—
It's myself, not my getup that's weird."

—Norman R. Jaffray

Curious Charlie

C is for Curious Charlie,
Who lives on rice, oatmeal and barley.
　　He once wrote a sonnet
　　On his mother's best bonnet,
And he lets his hair grow long and snarley.

—Isabel Frances Bellows

Opportunity's Knock

"I have heard," said a maid of Montclair,
"Opportunity's step on the stair,
　　But I couldn't unlock
　　To its magical knock,
For I always was washing my hair."

—Morris Bishop

The Old Man of the Hague

There was an old man of the Hague,
Whose ideas were excessively vague;
   He built a balloon
   To examine the moon,
That deluded old man of the Hague.

—Edward Lear

A Young Lady of Oakham

There was a young lady of Oakham,
Who would steal your cigars and then soak 'em
   In honey and rum,
   And then smear 'em with gum,
So it wasn't a pleasure to smoke 'em.

—Author Unknown

Beulah Louise

A mother in old Alabama
Said: "I declare, what a clamor!
   Little Beulah Louise
   Cut down those pine trees
With big brother's chisel and hammer!"

—William Jay Smith

A Young Girl of Asturias

There was a young girl of Asturias,
Whose temper was frantic and furious,
 She used to throw eggs
 At her grandmother's legs—
A habit unpleasant, but curious.

      —Author Unknown

A Young Fellow Named Shear

There was a young fellow named Shear
Who stuck a ball-point in his ear.
   As he punctured the drum
   He said, "That hurts some,
But the rest of the way through is clear."

                  —John Ciardi

Miss Hartley

A lady whose name was Miss Hartley
Understood most things only partly.
   When they said: "Get this straight,"
   She said: "What?—What?—What?—WAIT!"
So they had to give up with Miss Hartley.

                —William Jay Smith

Who's Next?

A clergyman told from his text
How Samson was scissored and vexed;
   Then a barber arose
   From his sweet Sunday doze,
Got rattled, and shouted, "Who's next?"

                —Author Unknown

Sir Bedivere Bors

Sir Bedivere Bors was a chivalrous knight;
His charger was proud and his armor was bright.
  But he grew very stout,
  So that when he rode out
He really presented a comical sight.

               —*Frederick B. Opper*

A Brave Knight

There was a brave knight of Lorraine,
Who hated to give people pain;
  "I'll skeer 'em," he said,
  "But I won't kill 'em dead!"
This noble young knight of Lorraine.

               —*Mary Mapes Dodge*

A Person of Note

There was an old stupid who wrote
The verses above that we quote;
  His want of all sense
  Was something immense,
Which made him a person of note.

               —*Walter Parke*

An Apple a Day

"I must eat an apple," said Link,
As he gobbled one down in a wink,
  "For an apple a day
  Keeps the doctor away—
And I just broke his window, I think."

—*Lee Blair*

Miss Tillie McLush

Annoying Miss Tillie McLush
Shopped early, avoiding the crush,
   Then brought everything back
   And demanded her jack
At the peak of the holiday rush.

               —Joseph S. Newman

A Limerick of Frankness

There was a frank lady of Dedham
Who whenever she thought of things, said 'em.
   When she opened her lips
   People took to their ships
And the sound of her accents just sped 'em.

               —X. Y. Z.

An Old Man by Salt Lake

There was an old man by Salt Lake
Who exclaimed when but partly awake:
   "Hi-di-diddle bum nickle
   Gum bubble tricycle!"
And they said: "Aw, go jump in the lake!"

               —William Jay Smith

A Young Man Who Loved Rain

There was a young man on a plain
Who wandered about in the rain.
  He said: "Well, what OF it?
  I LOVE it! I LOVE it!"
And he said so again and again.

            —William Jay Smith

A Mean Trick

He gave her some kind of elixir,
When she said to him, "I'm sixir."
   But it tasted so bad,
   That the lady got mad,
And said, "It's a very mean trixir."

                —Author Unknown

Naughty Young Nat

N is for naughty young Nat,
Who sat on his father's best hat.
   When they asked if he thought
   He had done as he ought,
He said he supposed 'twas the cat.

               —Isabel Frances Bellows

An Old Lady of Harrow

There was an old lady of Harrow
Who rode into church in a barrow.
   When she stuck in the aisle
   She said with a smaisle,
"They build these 'ere churches too narrow."

                —Author Unknown

Caught Stealing a Dahlia

A maiden caught stealing a dahlia,
Said, "Oh, you shan't tell on me, shahlia?"
   But the florist was hot,
   And he said, "Like as not,
They'll send you to jail, you bad gahlia."

                     —Author Unknown

A What-Is-It

There was an old man of high feather,
Who said, "I really can't tell whether
   I'm a man or a mouse,
   Or the roof of a house,
So much may depend on the weather."

              —Ruth McEnery Stuart and
                Albert Bigelow Paine

Beautiful Bella

B is for beautiful Bella,
Who brought back a borrowed umbrella.
   Though the tale you may doubt,
   I've no way to find out,
But I'll bet you that B is for Bella.

                     —Author Unknown

The Oil Lamp

There was an old person who said,
Pointing out the oil lamp on his head:
   "It perhaps does not pay
   During most of the day,
But it's helpful when reading in bed!"

               —William Jay Smith

A Young Lady Named Sue

There was a young lady named Sue,
Who wanted to catch the 2.02;
  Said the trainman, "Don't hurry
  Or flurry or worry;
It's a minute or two to 2.02."

—Author Unknown

A Young Lady of Crete

There was a young lady of Crete,
Who was so exceedingly neat,
  When she got out of bed
  She stood on her head,
To make sure of not soiling her feet.

—Author Unknown

An Old Man from Peru

There was an old man from Peru
Who dreamed he was eating his shoe.
  He awoke in the night
  And turned on the light
And found it was perfectly true.

—Author Unknown

An Old Miser Named Quince

A pointless old miser named Quince
Spent a lifetime in skinning his flints.
    When the last flint was skun
    He said, "Well, that's done."
And dropped dead, which he's been ever since.

—John Ciardi

MIND YOUR MANNERS

A Young Lady from Cork

There was a young lady from Cork
Who went at her soup with a fork.
  When her parents looked pained
  She proudly explained,
"That's the way they eat soup in New York."

—Ogden Nash

Jammy

There was a young hopeful named Sam
Who loved diving into the jam.
  When his mother said, "Sammy,
  Don't make yourself jammy,"
He said, "You're too late, ma, I am!"

—Elizabeth Ripley

A Young Curate of Kidderminster

There was a young curate of Kidderminster,
Who kindly, but firmly, chid a spinster,
  Because on the ice
  She said something not nice
When he quite inadvertently slid ag'inst her.

—Author Unknown

A Strong-Minded Lady

A strong-minded lady of Arden
Grows nothing but burrs in her garden;
  She tosses the burrs
  On passing chauffeurs,
And never begs anyone's pardon.

—Morris Bishop

Table Manners

When you turn down your glass it's a sign
That you're not going to take any wign.
  So turn down your plate
  When they serve things you hate,
And you'll often be asked to dign.

—James Montgomery Flagg

The Theater Hat

The girl with the theater hat
Went tripping along to the "mat."
   She cut off the view
   Of a dozen or two,
But she didn't care much about that.

              —Carolyn Wells

A Tidy Young Tapir

T was a tidy young tapir,
Who went out to bring in the paper;
   And when he came back
   He made no muddy track,
For he wiped his feet clean on the scraper.

              —Carolyn Wells

A Very Polite Man

A very polite man named Hawarden
Went out to plant flowers in his gawarden.
   If he trod on a slug,
   A worm or a bug,
He said: "My dear friend, I beg pawarden!"

Sarah Samantha

Here's sweet little Sarah Samantha,
Whose smile would have softened a panther.
   She lisped, I am told,
   But whoever might scold,
She *alwayth* returned a thoft anth'er!

                  —Author Unknown

PUNS— ATROCIOUS AND OTHERWISE

Serpentine Verse

Said an asp to an adder named Rhea,
"Ah, love is a sweet panacea!
*   You've got beauty and class*
*   Lovely snake in the grass!*
Oh, venom I next gonna see you?"

—Joseph S. Newman

The Twins

When twins came, their father, Dan Dunn,
Gave "Edward" as name to each son.
   When folks said, "Absurd!"
   He replied, "Ain't you heard
That two *Eds* are better than one?"

—*Berton Braley*

An Atrocious Pun

A major, with wonderful force,
Called out in Hyde Park for a horse.
  All the flowers looked round,
  But no horse could be found,
So he just rhododendron, of course.

—Author Unknown

Tra-La-Larceny

A heathen named Min, passing by
A pie-shop, picked up a mince pie.
  If you think Min a thief,
  Pray dismiss the belief:
The mince pie that Min spied was Min's pie.

—Oliver Herford

Sole-Hungering Camel

A camel, with practical views
On the nutritive value of shoes,
  To the mosque would repair
  While the folks were at prayer,
Little dreaming their souls they would lose.

—Oliver Herford

The Smart Little Bear

Teacher Bruin said, "Cub, bear in mind,
Licking ink from your pen's not refined,
   And eating blotting paper
   Is another bad caper—"
"Not," said the cub, "when I'm ink-lined."

                    —*Mark Fenderson*

The Humorous Ant

Once a grasshopper (food being scant)
Begged an ant some assistance to grant;
   But the ant shook his head,
   "I can't help you," he said,
"It's an uncle you need, not an ant."

                    —*Oliver Herford*

A Sightseer Named Sue

There was a sightseer named Sue
Who saw a strange beast at the zoo.
   When she asked, "Is it old?"
   She was smilingly told,
"It's not an old beast, but a gnu."

                    —*Author Unknown*

A Fellow Named Hall

There was a young fellow named Hall
Who fell in a spring, clothes and all.
   "It's amazing," said he,
   "And I don't really see
How I fell in the spring in the fall."

—*J. F. Wilson*

The Mendacious Mole

Said the mole: "You would never suppose
How far back my family goes.
  The first of my name
  From Normandy came
On William the Conqueror's nose."

                       —Oliver Herford

The Dragon

A dragon, who was a great wag,
Went out one day, pulling a drag.
  It filled us with awe,
  For who ever saw
A dragon a-draggin' a drag?

                    —Carolyn Wells

A Senator

A senator, Rex Asinorum,
Was needed to make up a quorum.
  So he flew down from Venice,
  Asked, "Who knows where my pen is?"
Then laconically scribbled, "I'm forum."

                    —Author Unknown

The Omnivorous Bookworm

Quoth the bookworm, "I don't care one bit
If writers have wisdom or wit;
   A volume must be
   Pretty dull to bore me
As completely as I can bore it."

—Oliver Herford

Such Foolish Old Dames

Two ladies with high social aims
(It wouldn't be fair to give names)
　　Saturated their rooms
　　With cologne and perfumes,
"For," said they, "we're Colonial Dames."

—Sam S. Stinson

*Pun*ishment

A father once said to his son,
"The next time you make up a pun,
　　Go out in the yard,
　　And kick yourself hard,
And I shall begin when you've done."

—Author Unknown

A Token of Attachment

The bachelor growls when his peace is
Disturbed by young nephews and nieces:
　　When their jam-bespread digits
　　Soil his trousers he fidgets,
Although they're preserving the creases.

—J. Adair Strawson

The Pleasing Gift

He received from some thoughtful relations
A spittoon with superb decorations.
   When asked was he pleased,
   He grimaced and wheezed,
"It's beyond all my expectorations."

                        —*Author Unknown*

Only Teasing

Said a cat, as he playfully threw
His wife down a well in Peru,
   "Relax, dearest Dora,
   Please don't be angora;
I only was artesian you."

                      —*Author Unknown*

A Strong Feeling for Poultry

A certain old party of Moultrie
Evinced a strong feeling for poultry.
   He knew all the hens,
   And roosters in pens,
And half of the biddies in Moultrie.

                      —*Roy Blount, Jr.*

Gnome Matter

There was once a dear little gnome
Who rode from his home on Cape Nome;
   Said a lady, "My dear,
   Do you know why you're here?"
He looked up and answered, "Why, no'm."

                    —Carolyn Wells

Raisin Bread

Here is the reply made by Benny
When he was questioned by Lenny:
   "Do you like raisin bread?"
   "I don't know," Benny said,
" 'Cause I never have tried raisin' any."

                    —Lee Blair

Sliding Scale

A salmon remarked to his mate:
"My dear, are you putting on weight?
   You were six and a half
   When you slipped from the gaff,
But they're claiming, right now, you were eight."

                    —Norman R. Jaffray

The Ounce of Detention

Once a pound-keeper chanced to impound
An ounce that was straying around.
   The pound-keeper straight
   Was fined for false weight,
Since he'd only one ounce in his pound.

              —Oliver Herford

Let X Equal Half

A mathematician named Bath
Let x equal half that he hath.
   He gave away y
   Then sat down to pi
And choked. What a sad afterMATH.

              —J. F. Wilson

THERE'S NOTHING
LIKE FOOD

A Young Lady of Munich

There was a young lady of Munich
Whose appetite simply was unich.
  "There's nothing like food,"
  She contentedly cooed,
As she let out a tuck in her tunich.

—Author Unknown

The Pious Young Priest

There once was a pious young priest
Who lived almost wholly on yeast;
  "For," he said, "it is plain
  We must all rise again,
And I want to get started, at least."

—*Author Unknown*

Ms. Minnie McFinney

Ms. Minnie McFinney, of Butte,
Fed always and only on frutte.
   Said she: "Let the coarse
   Eat of beef and of horse,
I'm a peach, and that's all there is tutte."

—*Author Unknown*

A Handy Guide

A handy old guide from the Bosphorous
Subsisted on sulphur and phosphorus.
   When out in the park
   He shone like a spark
And lighted the way clear across for us.

—*Author Unknown*

Rice and Mice

There was an old person of Ewell,
Who chiefly subsisted on gruel;
   But to make it more nice,
   He inserted some mice,
Which refreshed that old man of Ewell.

—*Edward Lear*

A Difficult Guest

Of inviting to dine, in Epirus,
A Centaur, a dame was desirous;
  But her servants demurred:
  "He's no man, beast, nor bird;
To feed such a freak you can't hire us."

—*Carroll Watson Rankin*

The Wild Boarder

His figure's not noted for grace;
You may not much care for his face;
   But a twenty-yard dash,
   When he hears the word "hash,"
He can take at a wonderful pace.

—Kenyon Cox

A Mock Miracle

There was a young waitress named Myrtle
Who carried a plate of mock turtle,
   When, strange to relate,
   She tripped, and the plate
That once was mock turtle turned turtle.

—Oliver Herford

From Number Nine, Penwiper Mews

From Number Nine, Penwiper Mews,
There is really abominable news:
   They've discovered a head
   In the box for the bread
But nobody seems to know whose.

—Edward Gorey

A Sporty Young Person

Said a sporty young person named Groat,
Who owned a black racehorse of note,
   "I consider it smart
   To dine à la carte,
But my horse always takes table d'oat."

                    —*Author Unknown*

A Professor Called Chesterton

There was a professor called Chesterton,
Who went for a walk with his best shirt on.
   Being hungry he ate it,
   But lived to regret it,
As it ruined for life his digesterton.

                    —*W. S. Gilbert*

Master of Arts

There once was a Master of Arts
Who was nuts upon cranberry tarts;
   When he'd eaten his fill,
   He was awfully ill,
But he still was a Master of Arts.

                    —*Cosmo Monkhouse*

Ignorant Ida

not using "there was..."

I is for Ignorant Ida,
Who doesn't know rhubarb from cider;
   Once she drank up a quart
   Which was more than she ought,
And it gave her queer feelings inside her.

               —*Isabel Frances Bellows*

Tea by the Sea

There was an old person of Putney,
Whose food was roast spiders and chutney,
   Which he took with his tea,
   Within the sight of the sea,
That romantic old person of Putney.

               —*Edward Lear*

Expert

A prominent lady in Brooking
Was a recognized genius at cooking.
   She could bake thirty pies
   All quite the same size
And tell which was which without looking.

               —*Author Unknown*

The Sick Shark

A chap has a shark up in Sparkill.
One day he discovered his shark ill;
 He said, "It's the man you et
 Over in Nanuet!
He'd make every beast in the Ark ill!"

     —Morris Bishop

A Hunter Named Shephard

They tell of a hunter named Shephard
Who was eaten for lunch by a lephard.
 Said the lephard, "Egad!
 You'd be tastier, lad,
If you had been salted and pephard."

     —Author Unknown

Hurtful Habits

There was an old person whose habits
Induced him to feed upon rabbits;
 When he'd eaten eighteen,
 He turned perfectly green,
Upon which he relinquished those habits.

     —Edward Lear

A Queer Fellow Named Woodin

There was a queer fellow named Woodin
Who always ate pepper with puddin';
   Till, one day, 'tis said,
   He sneezed off his head!
That imprudent old fellow named Woodin.

—*Edward Bradley*

An Old Man of Hawaii

There was an old man of Hawaii,
Who ate too much whale and shark paii;
   So quaffing some sperm-oil,
   He quitted life's turmoil
Without even saying, "Good-baii!"

—*Author Unknown*

Too Much

A greedy small lassie once said,
As she gobbled down slices of bread,
   "If I eat one more crust,
   I'm sure I will bust"—
At which point everyone fled.

—*Author Unknown*

An Odd Old Man in Hackensack

Absent-minded, in his shack,
An odd old man in Hackensack
   Was having supper rather late.
   He scratched the pancakes on his plate
And poured the syrup down his back

—Author Unknown

ON MUSIC
I DOTE

The Musical Lion

Said the Lion: "On music I dote,
But something is wrong with my throat,
When I practise a scale,
The listeners quail,
And flee at the very first note."

—Oliver Herford

A Coloratura Named Luna

A coloratura named Luna
Will lose her job soon if not sooner;
   She got sick on a dish
   Of casseroled fish
And now she can't carry the tuna.

                    —*J. F. Wilson*

A Thrifty Soprano

A thrifty soprano of Hingham
Designed her own dresses of gingham
   Which instead of big squares
   Bore opera airs,
So that when they wore out she could singham.

           —Ogden Nash

'Tis Strange

'Tis strange how the newspapers honor
A creature that's called prima donna.
   They say not a thing
   Of how she can sing
But write reams of the clothes she has on her.

           —Eugene Field

The Old Man with a Gong

There was an old man with a gong
Who bumped at it all the day long;
   But they called out, "Oh, law,
   You're a horrid old bore!"
So they smashed that old man with a gong.

           —Edward Lear

A Sensitive Man

There's a sensitive man in Toms River
Whom Beethoven causes to quiver;
   The aesthetic vibration
   Brings soulful elation
And also is fine for the liver.

                 —*Morris Bishop*

An Old Person of Tring

There was an old person of Tring
Who, when somebody asked her to sing,
   Replied, "Isn't it odd?
   I can never tell *God*
Save the Weasel from *Pop Goes the King!*"

                —*Author Unknown*

The Ichthyosaurus

An extinct old ichthyosaurus
Once offered to sing in a chorus;
   But the rest of the choir
   Were obliged to retire,
His voice was so worn and sonorous.

                —*Author Unknown*

A Nuisance at Home

Bill learned to play tunes on a comb
And became such a nuisance at homb,
   That Ma spanked him and said
   "Shall I put you to baid?"
And he cheerfully answered her, "Nomb."

                        —Author Unknown

Our Vicar

Our Vicar is good Mr. Inge
One evening he offered to sing,
   So we asked him to stoop,
   Put his head in a loop,
And pulled at each end of the string.

          —Author Unknown

Operatic Olivia

O's Operatic Olivia,
Who visits her aunt in Bolivia.
   She can sing to high C—
   But, between you and me,
They don't care for that in Bolivia.

          —Isabel Frances Bellows

Hit Tune

There was a composer named Bong
Who composed a new popular song.
   It was simply the croon
   Of a lovesick baboon,
With occasional thumps on the gong.

          —Author Unknown

The Misapprehended Goose

One evening a goose, for a treat,
For the opera purchased a seat.
   At the very first line
   She exclaimed, "How divine!"
And for hissing was thrown in the street.

                 —Oliver Herford

The Young Lady of Tyre

There was a young lady of Tyre,
Who swept the loud chords of a lyre;
   At the sound of each sweep,
   She enraptured the deep,
And enchanted the city of Tyre.

                —Edward Lear

SCHOOLISH, OR FOOLISH

from ON READING

"Curiosity's not in me head,"
Said a lazy young fellow named Ted,
  "So I ain't gonna look
  In your silly ole book—
I'm just gonna stay stupid instead."

                    —Myra Cohn Livingston

A Well-Informed Wight

W's a well-informed wight
Who loves to set everyone right,
   If a word you misspell
   Or misquote—he will swell
With chastened and holy delight.

              —Oliver Herford

Spell It

You have to be brainy, not drippy,
To learn how to spell Mississippi.
   The i's, p's, and s's
   Take knowing, not guesses.
(I think they are meant to be trippy.)

              —Author Unknown

A Warning

I know a young girl who can speak
French, German, and Latin and Greek.
   I see her each day,
   And it grieves me to say
That her English is painfully weak!

              —Mary A. Webber

A Quoter

Q is a quoter who'll cite
His favorite authors all night.
  Tho' glowing with thought,
  Like the moon he is naught
But a second-hand-dealer in light.

—Oliver Herford

The Fabulous Wizard of Oz

The fabulous wizard of Oz
Retired from business becoz
  What with up-to-date science
  To most of his clients
He wasn't the wiz that he woz.

—Author Unknown

At a Modernist School

At a modernist school in Park Hill
The children cause parents a chill
  By using their tools
  And their freedom from rules
In constructing a workable still.

—Morris Bishop

A Wild Worm

W was a wild worm,
All day he did nothing but squirm,
  They sent him to school,
  But he broke every rule,
And left at the end of the term.

—Carolyn Wells

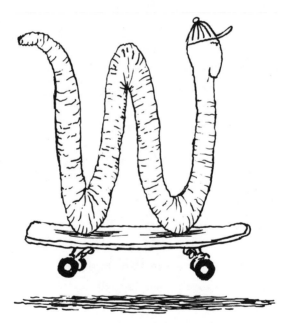

No Talking Shop

A schoolma'am of much reputation
In her steamer chair took up her station,
   And when asked could she tell
   How some word they should spell,
She said, "Yes, but not during vacation!"

                        —Minnie Leona Upton

On Reading: Four Limericks

"Curiosity's not in me head,"
Said a lazy young fellow named Ted,
   "So I ain't gonna look
   In your silly ole book—
I'm just gonna stay stupid instead."

              2.

If you don't know the meaning of *snook*
Or of *snaffle* or *rhombus* or *rukh*,
   If you're curious how
   To tell *dhoti* from *dhow*,
Get yourself up—and go find a book!

3.

If you're apt to be ravenous, look
All about you for signs of a book,
   Grab it up, eat the words,
   Take the whey from the curds,
And you'll end up digesting the book!

4.

A young person of precious precocity
Once informed us with vaunting verbosity,
   "I've received education
   Through my long lucubration,
Not to mention a coy curiosity."

               —*Myra Cohn Livingston*

BELL CORDS AND OTHER FINERY

Uncertain What to Wear

A matron well known in Montclair
Was never quite sure what to wear.
Once when very uncertain
She put on a lace curtain
And ran a bell cord through her hair.

— William Jay Smith

Good Thinking

There was, in the village of Patton
A chap who at church kept his hat on.
  "If I wake up," he said,
  "With my hat on my head,
"I'll know that it hasn't been sat on."

                    —Author Unknown

A Thrifty Young Fellow

A thrifty young fellow of Shoreham
Made brown paper trousers and woreham.
  He looked nice and neat
  Till he bent in the street
To pick up a pin, then he toreham.

—*Author Unknown*

The Eternal Feminine

Said the spider, in tones of distress:
"As a spinster I'm not a success.
  Though I toil and I spin
  And I work myself thin,
I never can have a new dress."

—*Oliver Herford*

An Old Man of Toulon

There was an old man of Toulon
Who never had anything on.
  When they said: "Wear some clothes!"
  He inquired: "What are those?"
So they chased that man out of Toulon.

—*William Jay Smith*

A Young Lady of Wilts

There was a young lady of Wilts,
Who walked to the Highlands on stilts.
   When they said, "Oh, how shocking!
   To show so much stocking,"
She answered, "Well, how about kilts?"

        —Author Unknown

High and Low

A boot and a shoe and a slipper
Lived once in a cobbler's row;
   But the boot and the shoe
   Would have nothing to do
With the slipper, because she was low.

But the king and the queen and their daughter
On the cobbler chanced to call;
   And as neither the boot
   Nor the shoe would suit
The slipper went off to the ball.

        —John Banister Tabb

IT WAS LOVE AT FIRST SIGHT

Church Bells

Said a fellow from North Philadelphia
To his girl, "When I saw ya, I fellphia.
  It was love at first sight,
  But 'twill last, honor bright,
Till the church bells are ringing a knellphia."

—Berton Braley

A Young Man on a Journey

A young man on a journey had met her,
And tried just his hardest to get her,
   He knelt at her feet—
   Said: "I'd die for you sweet,"
And she cruelly told him he'd better.

—Author Unknown

A Vaporish Maiden

There's a vaporish maiden in Harrison
Who longed for the love of a Saracen;
   But she had to confine her
   Intent to a shriner,
Who suffers, I fear, by comparison.

—Morris Bishop

Lenora

There was a young man from Elnora,
Who married a girl called Lenora,
   But he had not been wed
   Very long, till he said,
"Oh, drat it! I've married a snorer!"

—Author Unknown

Moonshine

There was a young lady of Rheims,
There was an old poet of Gizeh,
He rhymed on the deepest and sweetest of themes,
She scorned all his efforts to please her:
    And he sighed, "Ah, I see
    She and sense won't agree."
So he scribbled her moonshine, mere moonshine, and
      she,
With jubilant screams, packed her trunk up in
      Rheims,
Cried aloud, "I am coming, O bard of my dreams!"
And was clasped in his bosom in Gizeh.

                —Walter de la Mare

Antonio

Antonio, Antonio,
Was tired of living alonio.
   He thought he would woo
   Miss Lissamy Lou,
Miss Lissamy Lucy Molonio.

Antonio, Antonio,
Rode off on his polo-ponio,
   He found the fair maid
   In a bowery shade,
A-sitting and knitting alonio.

Antonio, Antonio,
Said, "If you will be my sunio,
   I'll love you true,
   And I'll buy for you,
An icery-creamery conio!"

"Oh, nonio, Antonio!
You're far too bleak and bonio!
   And all that I wish,
   You singular fish,
Is that you will quickly begonio."

Antonio, Antonio,
He uttered a dismal moanio,
　　Then ran off and hid
　　(Or I'm told that he did)
In the Antarctical Zonio.

　　　　　　　—Laura E. Richards

SUCH SILLY MISTAKES

The Car's in the Hall

Said a lady beyond Pompton Lakes
"I do make such silly mistakes!
  Now the car's in the hall!
  It went right through the wall
When I mixed up the gas and the brakes."

—Morris Bishop

Miss Hocket

A young kangaroo, Miss Hocket,
Carried dynamite sticks in her pocket.
  By mistake a match
  Dropped into her hatch,
And Miss Hocket took off like a rocket.

—*Author Unknown*

An Old Man of the Nile

There was an old man of the Nile,
Who sharpened his nails with a file;
    Till he cut off his thumbs,
    And said calmly, "This comes—
Of sharpening one's nails with a file!"

                —Edward Lear

Stop!

A careless young driver, McKissen,
Just never would stop, look, and lissen.
    A train at great speed
    He gave not one heed.
Now lissen! McKissen is missen.

                —Lee Blair

The Proud Engine

A railway official at Crewe
Met an engine one day that he knew.
    Though he smiled and he bowed,
    That engine was proud,
It cut him—it cut him in two!

                —Author Unknown

A Fatal Mistake

There was an old man of Peru,
Who watched his wife making a stew;
   But once by mistake,
   In a stove she did bake
That unfortunate man of Peru.

                  —Edward Lear

Zephyr

A farmer once called his cow "Zephyr";
She seemed such an amiable heifer.
   When the farmer drew near,
   She kicked off his ear,
Which made him considerably dephyr.

              —Author Unknown

The Careless Zookeeper

A careless zookeeper named Blake
Fell into a tropical lake.
   Said a fat alligator
   A few minutes later,
"Very nice, but I still prefer steak."

              —Author Unknown

Crockett

There was a young person named Crockett
Who attached himself to a rocket.
   He flew out through space
   At such a great pace
That his pants flew out of his pocket.

—William Jay Smith

Bruno

A jolly young artist called Bruno
Went to sketch in the bright month of June-O.
  On the banks of the Nile,
  Where a huge crocodile
Quickly tucked him away in his—"you know!"

—*Author Unknown*

Fire!

A new servant maid named Maria,
Had trouble in lighting the fire.
  The wood being green,
  She used gasoline.
Her position by now is much higher!

—*Author Unknown*

A Certain Young Gourmet

A certain young gourmet of Crediton
Took some pâté de foie gras and spread it on
  A chocolate biscuit
  Then murmured, "I'll risk it.
His tomb bears the date that he said it on.

—*Charles Cuthbert Inge*

95

The Inquisitive Leopard

A leopard when told that benzine
Removed spots and imparted a sheen,
  Just to try, drank a stein!
  Next moment no sign
Of a spot (or a leopard) was seen.

                  —Oliver Herford

An Old Person of Cromer

There was an old person of Cromer
Who stood on one leg to read Homer.
  When he found he grew stiff,
  He jumped over the cliff,
Which concluded that person of Cromer.

                  —Edward Lear

✓ A Lady Track Star

A lady track star from Toccoa
Once caught her foot in a lawnmoa.
  She yelled bloody murder,
  But nobody hearder.
She survived—sadder, wiser and sloa.

                —Roy Blount, Jr.

Clumsy

A clumsy young laddie was Mulligan.
He recently acted quite dulligan.
   He climbed a wall
   Then managed to fall
And landed *ker-plunk* on his skulligan.

               —*J. B. Lee*

Ouch!

A careless young lad down in Natchez
Burned his trousers from playing with matchez.
   To this careless young lad,
   "Bend down," said his dad.
On the seat of his pants he wears patchez.

             —*Author Unknown*

On the Wrong Side

A Conservative, out on his motor,
Ran over a Radical voter.
   "Thank goodness," he cried,
   "He was on the wrong side,
So I don't blame myself one iota."

             —*A. W. Webster*

The Peach

There once was a peach on a tree,
The fairest you ever did see,
   But it ripened too fast,
   Till it fell down at last,
And turned to a squash! O dear me!

Abbie Farwell Brown

A Housewife

A housewife called out with a frown
When surprised by some callers from town,
   "In a minute or less
   I'll slip on a dress"—
But she slipped on the stairs and came down.

—Author Unknown

A Patriot

A patriot, living at Ewell,
Found his bonfire wanted more fuel,
   So he threw in Uncle James
   To heighten the flames,
A measure effective though cruel.

—Langford Reed

Edser

There was a young soldier called Edser
When wanted was always in bed sir:
  One morning at one,
  They fired the gun
And Edser, in bed sir, was dead sir.

—Spike Milligan

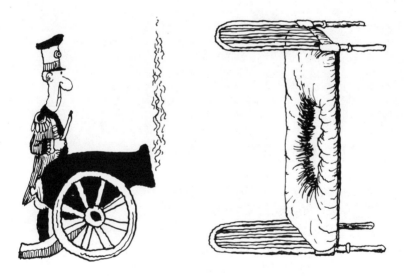

CAN YOU READ THESE? THEY'RE ESPECIALLY TRICKY

Dirt Dumping

A man hired by John Smith and Co.
Loudly declared that he'd tho.
   Men that he saw
   Dumping dirt near his store.
The drivers, therefore, didn't do.

          —Mark Twain

A Helpful Nurse

A handsome young gent down in Fla.
Collapsed in a hospital ca.
    A young nurse from Me.
    Sought to banish his pe.
And shot him. Now what could be ha.?

—Author Unknown

A Young School Mistress

A pretty young school mistress named Beauchamp,*
Said, "These awful boys how shall I teauchamp?
    For they will not behave,
    Although I look grave
And with tears in my eyes I beseauchamp."

—Author Unknown

Two Jays at St. Louis

A guy asked two jays at St. Louis
What kind of an Indian the Souis.
    They said: "We're no en-
    Cyclopedia by hen!"
Said the guy: "If you fellows St. Whouis?"

—Ferdinand G. Christgau

---

*In Great Britain, Beauchamp is pronounced Beecham.

The Sioux

When they go out walking the Sioux
March single-file—never by tioux—
   And by "blazing" the trees
   Can return at their ease,
And their way through the forest ne'er lioux.

All new-fashioned boats he eschioux,
And uses his birch-bark canioux;
   These are handy and light,
   And, inverted at night,
Give shelter from storms and from dyioux.

—Author Unknown

A Young Lady from Delaware

There was a young lady from Del.
Who was most undoubtedly wel.
   That to dress for a masque
   Wasn't much of a tasque,
But she cried, "What the heck will my fel.?"

—Author Unknown

A Hearty Cook

A hearty old cook of Lithonia
Intensively forces food onia;
   And when you're about
   To quit she will shout
"I bet I can eat a lot monia."

               —Roy Blount, Jr.

St. Thomas

A bright little maid in St. Thomas
Discovered a suit of pajhomas.
   Said the maiden: "Well, well!
   What they are I can't tell;
But I'm sure that these garments St. Mhomas."

         —Ferdinand G. Christgau

An All-American Guard

When an All-American gd.,
Whose tackles had always been hd.,
   Faced earning a living
   He found he'd been giving
His studies too little regd.

            —Author Unknown

A Lady Named Psyche

A beautiful lady named Psyche
Is loved by a fellow named Yche.
   One thing about Ych
   The lady can't lych
Is his beard, which is dreadfully spyche.

                —Author Unknown

Money Makes the Marriage

Said a maid, "I will marry for lucre,"
And her scandalized ma almost shucre;
   But when the chance came,
   And she told the good dame,
I notice she did not rebuchre.

        —From the St. Louis Post Dispatch

The Lost Girl

An old couple living in Gloucester
Had a beautiful girl, but they loucester;
   She fell from a yacht,
   And never the spacht
Could be found where the cold waves had toucester.

                —Author Unknown

The Musical Maiden

On pianos and organs she lbs.,
Making strange and mysterious sds.,
   And the policeman calls out
   To see what she's about,
As he goes on his lone nightly rds.

              —Author Unknown

The One-Legged Colonel

A distinguished old one-legged colonel
Once started to edit a jolonel;
   But soon, quite disgusted,
   Gave up—he was busted—
And cried, "The expense is infolonel!"

              —Author Unknown

Persuasive Go-Gebtor

A merchant addressing a debtor
Remarked in the course of his lebtor
   That he chose to suppose
   A man knose what he ose
And the sooner he pays it the bebtor.

        —R. C. in the Springfield Union

A Lady Who Lived at Bordeaux

A lady who lived at Bordeaux,
Had a corn on her right little teaux;
   She borrowed a razor,
    For her skill we must praise her,
For the corn is gone (so is her teaux).

                —Author Unknown

Wilhelmj

Oh, King of the fiddle, Wilhelmj,
If truly you love me just tellmj;
   Just answer my sigh
    By a glance of your eye,
Be honest, and don't try to sellmj.

With rapture your music did thrillmj;
With pleasure supreme did it fillmj;
   And if I could believe
    That you meant to deceive—
Wilhelmj, I think it would killmj.

              —Robert J. Burdette

Nothing More Than a Sister

A precocious, impulsive young Mr.
Was in love with a girl—and he kr.
   Said she, "Sir, go slow!
   For I'll have you know
I'm to you nothing more than a sr.

          —*From the* Tacoma News

The Amorous *Señor*

See that *señor* so amorous and menacing
Kiss the young *señorita* while tennising!
   Her duenna, upset,
   Comes and sits on the net—
The duenna won't let him duennacing!

          —*Ogden Nash*

Once a Frenchman

Once a Frenchman who'd promptly said "oui"
To some ladies who'd asked him if houi
   Cared to drink, threw a fit
   Upon finding that it
Was a tipple no stronger than toui.

          —*Author Unknown*

"O-U-G-H-"; or, The Cross Farmer

A farmer's boy, starting to plough,
Once harnessed an ox with a cough;
 But the farmer came out,
 With furious shout,
And told him he didn't know hough.

In a manner exceedingly rough,
He proceeded to bluster and blough;
 He scolded and scowled,
 He raved and he howled,
And declared he'd have none of such stough.

At length, with a growl and a cough,
He dragged the poor boy to the trough,
 And ducking him in
 Till wet to his chin,
Discharged him and ordered him ough.

And now my short story is through—
And I will not assert that it's trough,
 But it's chiefly designed
 To impress on your mind
What wonders our spelling can dough.

And I hope you will grant that although
It may not be the smoothest in flough,
   It has answered its end
   If it only shall tend
To prove what I meant it to shough.

—*D. S. Martin*

WRITE THE LAST
LINE YOURSELF

Know Your True Worth

Said a rooster, "I'd have you all know
I am nearly the whole of the show;
   Why, the sun every morn
   Gets up with the dawn
. . . . . .

Tired of Waiting

There was a young fellow from Tyne
Put his head on the South-Eastern Line;
    But he died of ennui,
    For the 5:53
•   •   •   •   •

Cider Inside Her

There was a young lady of Ryde
Who ate a green apple and died.
    The apple fermented
    Inside the lamented
•   •   •   •   •

Meet Neat Rosie De Fleet

A girl I know, Rosie De Fleet,
Is so very unusually neat
    She washes all day
    To keep microbes away,
•   •   •   •   •

Squeaky Shoes

There was a young lady from Ayr
Tried to sneak out of church during prayer
    But the squeak of her shoes
    Loudly broadcast the news
•   •   •   •   •

Bad Manners

An ambitious, and young, Ph.D.,
Got a bid, one day, to a T,
    At the Y.M.C.A.
    And he felt like a J,
•   •   •   •   •

The Curate's Cat

There was a kind curate of Kew,
Who kept a large cat in a pew;
    There he taught it each week
    A new letter of Greek,
•   •   •   •   •

A Jolly Young Chemist

A jolly young chemistry tough,
While mixing a compounded stuff,
  Dropped a match in the vial,
  And after a while—
•   •   •   •   •

Invitation to a Fish

A fellow who lived on the Rhine
Saw a fish that he wanted to dhine,
    But how to invite him?—
    "Ah," he said, "I will write him!"
•   •   •   •   •

The Kept Secret

There was an old codger of Broome,
Who kept a baboon in his room.
    "It reminds me," he said,
    "Of a friend who is dead,"
•   •   •   •   •

Maid of Manila

There was a young maid of Manila,
Whose favorite cream was vanilla,
    But sad to relate,
    Though you piled up her plate,
•   •   •   •   •

An Old Fellow from Cleathe

There was an old fellow from Cleathe
Who sat on his set of false teeth.
   Said he, with a start,
   "Oh, no! Bless my heart!

•   •   •   •   •

Index of Authors

Index of Titles

Index of First Lines

About the Compilers

A coauthor of the *Index to Poetry for Children and Young People,* John E. Brewton has compiled many distinguished anthologies of poetry and verse for children. Born in Brewton, Alabama, Dr. Brewton was graduated from Howard College in Birmingham, Alabama, and received his M.A. and Ph.D. degrees from George Peabody College for Teachers in Nashville, Tennessee. He is now Professor of English, Emeritus, at George Peabody College for Teachers, and makes his home in Kingston Springs, Tennessee.

Lorraine Acker Blackburn coauthored with John E. Brewton and G. Meredith Blackburn III the *Index to Poetry for Children and Young People* (1970–1975), published in 1978. She also worked on *Of Quarks, Quasars, and Other Quirks: Quizzical Poems for the Supersonic Age,* published in 1977. She is a graduate of Stuart Hall in Staunton, Virginia, and attended Vanderbilt University in Nashville, Tennessee, and George Peabody College for Teachers, from which she received a degree in Special Education. She has taught in the Metropolitan Nashville school system for the past six years.

About the Illustrator

Fernando Krahn was born in Chile and has been drawing since he was a child. His cartoons have appeared in *Esquire, The New Yorker, Atlantic Monthly,* and other publications and have been collected in an anthology called *The Possible Worlds of Fernando Krahn.* The recipient of a Guggenheim Fellowship for his work in film animation, he is also the author and illustrator of many books for children, including *April Fools, Giant Footsteps in the Snow,* and *Sebastian and the Mushroom.* Mr. Krahn lives in Spain with his wife and three children.